$\mathcal{A}$DVENT *and* $\mathcal{C}$HRISTMAS $\mathcal{W}$ISDOM
—— *from* ——
SAINT
VINCENT
DE PAUL

*A*DVENT *and* *C*HRISTMAS *W*ISDOM

—— *from* ——

SAINT VINCENT
DE PAUL

Daily Scripture and Prayers Together
With Saint Vincent de Paul's Own Words

Compiled by John E. Rybolt, CM

Liguori
LIGUORI, MISSOURI

Imprimi Potest: Harry Grile, CSsR
Provincial, Denver Province, The Redemptorists

Published by Liguori Publications
Liguori, Missouri 63057

To order, call 800-325-9521
www.liguori.org

Library of Congress Cataloging-in-Publication Data
Advent and Christmas wisdom from St. Vincent de Paul : daily scripture and prayers together with St. Vincent de Paul's own words / John E. Rybolt. — 1st ed.
    p. cm.
    ISBN 978-0-7648-2010-6
    1. Advent—Prayers and devotions. 2. Christmas—Prayers and devotions. 3. Catholic Church—Prayers and devotions. I. Rybolt, John E. II. Vincent de Paul, Saint, 1581-1660. Selections. English.
    BX2170.A4A37 2012
    242'.33—dc23

                                                                2012013225

Liguori Publications, a nonprofit corporation, is an apostolate of the Redemptorists. To learn more about the Redemptorists, visit Redemptorists.com.

Printed in the United States of America
16 15 14 13 12 / 5 4 3 2 1
First Edition

Contents

Introduction

Saint Vincent de Paul (1580/81–1660) is commonly called the Saint or Apostle of Charity. In search of a comfortable living, he became a priest at a very young age, but his attitude changed as he encountered the poor. For him, the poor and most abandoned were the privileged site for encountering the Lord. From his thirties on, he dedicated himself to their care.

In art he is often depicted with children, but his true concentration was evangelization to the poor of all ages. He founded two communities to carry on this work: the Congregation of the Mission (called Vincentians or Lazarists) and the Daughters of Charity. For them he developed a new, even radical, style of life. The sisters were to dress in secular clothing and live an active apostolate. Like Vincent de Paul, the priests and brothers were contemplatives in action.

We're fortunate to have much of his correspondence. Also valuable are his talks, or "conferences," given to both congregations. This book endeavors to present his thoughts in a way that can lead to a deeper relationship with God, a better appreciation of our own Christian life, and greater love for all, especially the poor.

The meditative texts used here are taken from conferences to his confreres. Vincent de Paul didn't often reflect on Advent and

Christmas, but he was keenly aware of the greater issues of our life in Christ, whose incarnation is celebrated at this season.

You can use this book in several ways. You can simply read the material each day, or you can also write ideas or resolutions in a journal. In rereading your notes later, you'll find added strength in the inspirations you receive.

How to Use This Book

Advent—that period of great anticipatory joy—is a time of preparation for the celebration of Christ's arrival in Bethlehem as a helpless infant. In the Western liturgy, Advent begins four Sundays prior to December 25—the Sunday closest to November 30, which is the feast of Saint Andrew, one of Jesus' first disciples.

The annual commemoration of Christ's birth begins the Christmas cycle of the liturgical year—a cycle that runs from Christmas day to the Baptism of the Lord. In keeping with the unfolding of the message of the liturgical year, this book is designed to be used from the first Sunday of Advent through twelve days of the Christmas cycle, or until January 6.

The four weeks of Advent are often thought of as symbolizing the four ways Christ comes into the world: (1) his birth as a helpless infant; (2) his arrival in the hearts of believers; (3) his death; and (4) his arrival on Judgment Day.

Because Christmas falls on a different day of the week each year, the fourth week of Advent seldom lasts a full week—it is abruptly, joyously, and solemnly abrogated by the annual coming of Christ at Christmas. Christ's Second Coming will also one day abruptly interrupt our sojourn here on Earth.

In this book, each day's passages begin with the words of Saint Vincent de Paul. Next is a related excerpt from Scripture, which is followed by a prayer built on the ideas from the two preceding passages. Finally, an Advent or Christmas action suggests ways to apply the messages to daily life.

Because the length of Advent varies, this book includes material for twenty-eight days. These daily readings make up Part I. You can skip the "extra" entries, or you can fit them all in by doubling up on days or weekends.

Part II begins with Christmas Day and contains materials for twelve days of the Christmas season.

Part III proposes two optional formats for using each day as part of a longer liturgical observance similar to Night Prayer, combined with a version of the Office of Readings. The purpose of these readings is to enrich the Advent/Christmas/Epiphany season of the liturgical year and set up a means by which individuals, families, or groups can observe the true meaning of the season.

PART I

~

READINGS

for

ADVENT

DAY 1

Meditation

*M*editation is a sermon we preach to ourselves to convince us of the need we have to turn to God and to cooperate with His grace in order to uproot vices from our soul and implant virtues in it.

CONFERENCE 68

SCRIPTURE

In those days he departed to the mountain to pray, and he spent the night in prayer to God.

LUKE 6:12

The Spirit drove him out into the desert, and he remained in the desert for forty days, tempted by Satan. He was among wild beasts, and the angels ministered to him.

MARK 1:12–13

PRAYER

Lord Jesus, you spent whole nights in fasting and prayer, in loving communion with your Father. Help me as I begin this quiet time of Advent to imitate your devotion to prayer and recollection. Give me the inner silence to grow in mindfulness of your love and care. When Christmas comes, may I celebrate the anniversary of your birth with greater devotion.

ADVENT ACTION

In today's busy world with our multiple responsibilities, it's difficult to find time even for a few minutes of meditation, let alone devote whole nights in prayer like Jesus did. Saint Vincent's faithfulness to meditation throughout his adult life shows in his insights and practical charity. Make a special resolution at the beginning of this Advent season to spend some quiet time preaching a sermon to yourself. Nourish it with reading, particularly from the New Testament.

DAY 2

Prudence in Speech

*P*rudence helps us to speak wisely and at the right time, caus- ing us to converse discreetly and judiciously of things that are good in their nature and circumstances and to keep silent about and suppress those that are contrary to God or which may harm the neighbor or tend to our own praise or to some other bad end.

CONFERENCE 35

SCRIPTURE

Know this, my dear brothers: everyone should be quick to hear, slow to speak, slow to wrath, for the wrath of a man does not accomplish the righteousness of God. Therefore, put away all filth and evil excess and humbly welcome the word that has been planted in you and is able to save your souls.

JAMES 1:19–21

PRAYER

Holy Spirit, giver of all good gifts, grant me the grace of prudence in my speech. Help me control my urge to speak without thinking about how my words may wound others, especially those closest to me.

ADVENT ACTION

Ask yourself whether a particular conversation during the day hurt you in any way, and how this happened. Then examine the same conversation from the other side, and ask how your words may have hurt others. What should you do to avoid such unfortunate interactions?

DAY 3

Pilgrimage

*H*ave you ever gone on pilgrimage to some place of devotion? On entering it, we usually feel as if we're outside of ourselves, some finding themselves suddenly lifted up in God, others moved to devotion, others filled with respect and reverence for that holy place, and others have various good sentiments. What accounts for this? It's because the Spirit of God is there.

CONFERENCE 7

SCRIPTURE

I rejoiced when they said to me,
"Let us go to the house of the LORD."
And now our feet are standing
within your gates, Jerusalem.
Jerusalem, built as a city,
walled round about.
There the tribes go up,
the tribes of the LORD,
As it was decreed for Israel,
to give thanks to the name of the LORD.

PSALM 122:1–4

PRAYER

Almighty Father, grant me the grace to be ever more aware of your Holy Spirit when I'm in church or praying with others. Touch me deeply, move me, and transform me into the worshiper I should be, in spirit and in truth.

ADVENT ACTION

Take Saint Vincent's suggestion seriously during this Advent, and if possible visit a church of special devotion. Enter, sit quietly, breathe deeply, and sense the presence of God's Holy Spirit. Get in touch with others' devotion, their gestures, and their awareness of the Divine.

Advent Simplicity

*H*e strongly urged us to be simple, especially since, where simplicity existed, God, who was simplicity personified and totally one and who did not tolerate being of two minds, was found there; *cum simplicibus sermocinatio ejus* ["his conversation is with the simple"; see Proverbs 3:32].

CONFERENCE 16

SCRIPTURE

Behold, I am sending you like sheep in the midst of wolves; so be shrewd as serpents and simple as doves. But beware of people, for they will hand you over to courts and scourge you in their synagogues, and you will be led before governors and kings for my sake as a witness before them and the pagans. When they hand you over, do not worry about how you are to speak or what you are to say. You will be given at that moment what you are to say.

MATTHEW 10:16–19

PRAYER

God, loving Father and Creator, you are infinitely one, simple and whole. Your son Jesus taught us that quality of wholeness: never divided, never devious, never of two minds. Give me that strength to imitate him in my life. May my words be clear and simple, and may my attitudes likewise be stripped of whatever is devious.

ADVENT ACTION

Take a few minutes during the day to examine your approach to difficult situations, especially relationships you find difficult. What is your leading principle: being honest, direct, free of deceit, or being complex and dishonest? Do others trust you to tell the truth? If not, Advent is the time to clean out habits that are so unlike those of Jesus.

DAY 5

Gentleness

*T*o foresee the occasions when we might fail in gentleness, to think about what topics might provoke angry reactions, and form mentally in advance the acts of gentleness we intend to practice on all occasions.

CONFERENCE 47

SCRIPTURE

A mild answer turns back wrath,
but a harsh word stirs up anger.
The tongue of the wise pours out knowledge,
but the mouth of fools spews folly.
A soothing tongue is a tree of life,
but a perverse one breaks the spirit.

PROVERBS 15:1–2, 4

PRAYER

Gentle Savior, you taught that the gentle will inherit the earth. Grant me your virtue of gentleness, that I may be ever more like you and represent you in this world. Banish from me all that is harsh and angry, and heal the roots that sprout into sin in my life.

ADVENT ACTION

We bear the name *Christian* not because we belong to a club of Christians, but because we have been baptized in the name of Jesus Christ. We are a new creation and are bound to act in his name. Look at yourself today in a kind of spiritual mirror to see whether you have truly become Christlike. Examine this from the perspective of gentleness.

DAY 6

A Sense of Self

*N*o one should flatter himself, or be complacent, or have any self-esteem about [the good we accomplish], seeing that God works great things by His own means; but we should humble ourselves all the more and recognize that we're puny instruments that God deigns to use.

CONFERENCE 39

SCRIPTURE

"Give your servant, therefore, a listening heart to judge your people and to distinguish between good and evil. For who is able to give judgment for this vast people of yours?"

The Lord was pleased by Solomon's request. So God said to him: Because you asked for this—you did not ask for a long life for yourself, nor for riches, nor for the life of your enemies—but you asked for discernment to know what is right—I now do as you request. I give you a heart so wise and discerning that there has never been anyone like you until now, nor after you will there be anyone to equal you.

1 KINGS 3:9–12

PRAYER

Lord of all truth, I rejoice when I see your action in the world. Help me see myself as the object of your love, but may I never replace you with myself as the center of my world. May all that I accomplish begin only with your inspiration and continue with your loving care.

ADVENT ACTION

It's easy for us to attribute any good we accomplish to our intelligence, abilities, or good luck. It's much more difficult to see God's hand in it. Pick out one or two accomplishments that especially satisfy you and examine them for proof of God's loving providence. Thank God for these benefits— accomplished *through* you—and beg him to remove any sense of self-importance that clings to them.

DAY 7

Waiting for Healing

*L*et's reflect that infirmities and sufferings come from God. Death, life, health, sickness—all these come by order of His Providence and, no matter how they come, they're always for our benefit and salvation.

CONFERENCE 55

SCRIPTURE

Make friends with the doctor, for he is essential to you;
God has also established him in his profession.
From God the doctor has wisdom,
and from the king he receives sustenance.
God makes the earth yield healing herbs
which the prudent should not neglect;
He endows people with knowledge,
to glory in his mighty works,
My son, when you are ill, do not delay,
but pray to God, for it is he who heals.

SIRACH 38:1–2, 4, 6, 9

PRAYER

Father of all, I believe and profess your love for me, but I sometimes waver when I am surrounded by sickness and death. With the light of faith, may I know and grasp your hand in these dark moments. See me through to healing and new life.

ADVENT ACTION

Read or watch news reports and try to absorb the amount of suffering that confronts us every day as thousands die or are gravely wounded. Put yourself in the place of the suffering victims and their loved ones and pray in their name for healing. Sometimes a photograph of such a person can help us raise that person to God.

DAY 8

Simple Meditation

*E*levat[e] our mind to God and [listen] to Him, because a single one of His words can do more than a thousand reasons and all the speculations of our understanding.

CONFERENCE 68

SCRIPTURE

O LORD, our Lord,

how awesome is your name through all the earth!

I will sing of your majesty above the heavens.

When I see your heavens, the work of your fingers,

the moon and stars that you set in place—

What is man that you are mindful of him,

and a son of man that you care for him?

PSALM 8:2, 4–5

PRAYER

Loving creator God, with one word you created all things and set the universe in motion. Help me hear the one word you will say to me today, and send your Holy Spirit to strengthen me to respond fully and completely. Your loving word is beyond my understanding, but I confess and proclaim your love.

ADVENT ACTION

For the whole time of human presence on the Earth, our ancestors have tried to outthink the Creator. In fact, as Saint Vincent urges with his usual clear vision, God is almighty. With one word, he can pierce our thoughts. Pick a favorite passage from Scripture, such as the Lord's Prayer (Matthew 6:9–15) or a beatitude from the Sermon on the Mount (Matthew 5:3–12). Read the passage several times and pray over it to hear the one word the Lord has for you today.

DAY 9

The Effects of Charity

*G*ood or bad qualities are spread exteriorly, especially charity, which, in itself, is contagious and produces charity. A heart truly on fire and animated with this virtue makes its ardor felt; and everything in a charitable man breathes and preaches charity.

CONFERENCE 59

SCRIPTURE

I kneel before the Father, from whom every family in heaven and on earth is named, that he may grant you in accord with the riches of his glory to be strengthened with power through his Spirit in the inner self, and that Christ may dwell in your hearts through faith; that you, rooted and grounded in love, may have strength to comprehend with all the holy ones what is the breadth and length and height and depth, and to know the love of Christ that surpasses knowledge, so that you may be filled with all the fullness of God.

EPHESIANS 3:14–19

PRAYER

Lord Jesus, through your life, death, and rising, you taught us the truth of charity, evident at every moment of your life. Fill me with that same charity, that I may always love what you loved and practice what you taught. May your charity in me spread to those who live without experiencing it.

ADVENT ACTION

Advent is a wonderful time to back away from activities that keep us focused on our own interests and that may turn us away from practicing charity to others. According to the old saying, charity begins at home, so today look for an opportunity to practice Jesus' charity in your family circle. Many acts of charity can, in Saint Vincent's experience, inflame the heart and warm others with love for God.

DAY 10

Prudence

*P*rudence of the flesh and the world has for its goal the pursuit of honors, pleasures, and wealth; therefore, it's totally opposed to Christian prudence and simplicity, which distance us from these misleading benefits, helping us to espouse solid, lasting benefits.

CONFERENCE 35

SCRIPTURE

"If you wish to be perfect, go, sell what you have and give to [the] poor, and you will have treasure in heaven. Then come, follow me." When the young man heard this statement, he went away sad, for he had many possessions.

MATTHEW 19:21–22

PRAYER

Lord Jesus, in your life I see none of the pursuit of worldly pleasures, fame, and wealth. Give me the light I need to imitate you and honor your prudence and simplicity. May you alone be my only reward in this life and the next.

ADVENT ACTION

Think about money today. In the calmness of the Advent season, ask yourself where your heart is on this question. What kind of example do you set for others who depend on you? What lessons do they learn from your words and actions concerning worldly goods? If you feel a call to repent, single out a person or charity that could benefit from your generosity.

DAY 11

How to Read for Prayer

*I*f they haven't studied, advise them to take their book in hand, pause at a particular consideration, and dwell on it for a long time, in order to allow it to permeate the memory so that they'll remember it; to permeate the understanding so that they may understand the truth; and lastly, the will, so that they may become attached to it.

CONFERENCE 107A

SCRIPTURE

By wisdom a house is built,
by understanding it is established;
And by knowledge its rooms are filled
with every precious and pleasing possession.
The wise are more powerful than the strong,
and the learned, than the mighty.

PROVERBS 24:3–5

PRAYER

Ever-living God, your words to us in holy Scripture have nourished the Church, strengthened the weak, emboldened the martyrs, and illuminated your saints. May I, too, have an outpouring of your Spirit to hear your words proclaimed and to study these saving texts. Give me the insight I need to be nourished, strengthened, emboldened, and illuminated.

ADVENT ACTION

Saint Vincent advised his brothers to read the holy Scriptures daily and to adore the truths contained therein. On first developing the habit of reading and studying the Bible, many people want to plunge into the beginning and read straight through. A better approach is to begin with Jesus: Pick a Gospel and read it carefully. Make notes, ask questions, and summarize what you learn. What better time than Advent to dig more deeply into the Word of God?

DAY 12

The Faults of Others

*W*e mustn't be surprised to see others commit faults because, just as it's characteristic of brambles and thistles to be prickly, it's characteristic of the corrupt nature of man to fail.

CONFERENCE 60C

SCRIPTURE

Put on then, as God's chosen ones, holy and beloved, heartfelt compassion, kindness, humility, gentleness, and patience, bearing with one another and forgiving one another, if one has a grievance against another; as the Lord has forgiven you, so must you also do.

COLOSSIANS 3:12–13

PRAYER

Dear Lord, while I try to follow your way, I still find myself hemmed in on all sides with the effects of human weakness, my own first of all, and then others'. Pour your healing balm over my soul, that I might grow in peace amid evil. Help me be understanding and forgiving of others, and give them the strength to bear with me in my moments of weakness.

ADVENT ACTION

Without being smug about our attempts to follow the Lord, we can still be troubled at the prickly "brambles and thistles" Saint Vincent mentioned. To gain some balance, write down the faults or difficult behavior of one or two others who trouble you most. Then, write down next to them some of your behaviors that need healing and redemption. Offer them all to the Lord, and beg for healing.

DAY 13

Prayer and Action

*L*et us love God, brothers, let us love God, but let it be with the strength of our arms and the sweat of our brows; for very often many acts of love of God, of devotion, and of other similar affections and interior practices of a tender heart, although very good and desirable, are, nevertheless, very suspect if they don't translate into the practice of effective love.

CONFERENCE 25

SCRIPTURE

We were gentle among you, as a nursing mother cares for her children. With such affection for you, we were determined to share with you not only the gospel of God, but our very selves as well, so dearly beloved had you become to us. You recall, brothers, our toil and drudgery. Working night and day in order not to burden any of you, we proclaimed to you the gospel of God.

1 THESSALONIANS 2:7–9

PRAYER

Father, Lord of heaven and Earth, we know you hear our prayers. Send me your Holy Spirit to purify the movements of my heart and imagination, that I may offer you pure worship. May my prayers also continue beyond words into deeds and actions that demonstrate your love and paternal care.

ADVENT ACTION

Saint Vincent's formulation of prayer and action is a classic of spiritual teaching. Take some time to read it several times and then, after interior prayer involving the gift of yourself to God, decide on a concrete and specific action that will make evident your internal and external commitments.

Self-discipline

he holy Doctors say that the first step for a person who wants to acquire virtue is to become the master of his mouth. Now, the mouth has the mastery over persons who give it what it asks for. What a disorder! They're its servants, its slaves.

CONFERENCE 6

SCRIPTURE

Finally, brothers, whatever is true, whatever is honorable, whatever is just, whatever is pure, whatever is lovely, whatever is gracious, if there is any excellence and if there is anything worthy of praise, think about these things. Keep on doing what you have learned and received and heard and seen in me. Then the God of peace will be with you.

PHILIPPIANS 4:8–9

PRAYER

Lord, free me from the forms of slavery that surround me and which I have grown accustomed to. Make me like Jesus, free of all disorders, who spoke only to bless and heal.

ADVENT ACTION

After your work day, try to recall the words that came out almost automatically, without forethought. Were they words of blessing or cursing, wounding or healing? What is the source of the anger or frustration they reveal? Offer to God these inadvertent expressions of inner anger and ask quietly for healing.

DAY 15

Intercession for Priests

*T*here are also bad priests in the world, and I am the worst, the most unworthy, and the greatest sinner of all of them. But, on the other hand, there are also those who give high praise to God by the holiness of their lives.

CONFERENCE 6

SCRIPTURE

Every high priest is taken from among men and made their representative before God, to offer gifts and sacrifices for sins. He is able to deal patiently with the ignorant and erring, for he himself is beset by weakness and so, for this reason, must make sin offerings for himself as well as for the people.

HEBREWS 5:1–3

PRAYER

Father, you have entrusted the sacraments of your Church to your priests. Although some have shown human weakness, please do not let that decrease my faith. Rather, strengthen it for my own loving service of your people, and strengthen your priests for the service of the Church.

ADVENT ACTION

We have heard about the all-too-human lives of priests. When you hear about their sins and failings, offer them to God and beg forgiveness for the priests. Reach out to priests, and offer your support in the way God leads you. Bless God for the good they are accomplishing.

DAY 16

Service for Priests

*H*ow fortunate you are, Messieurs, to spread the Spirit of God in those souls by your own devotion, gentleness, friendliness, modesty, and humility, and to serve God in the person of His greatest servants!

CONFERENCE 6

SCRIPTURE

Peter began to say to him, "We have given up everything and followed you." Jesus said, "Amen, I say to you, there is no one who has given up house or brothers or sisters or mother or father or children or lands for my sake and for the sake of the gospel who will not receive a hundred times more now in this present age...and eternal life in the age to come."

MARK 10:28–30

PRAYER

Jesus, great high priest, you have entrusted your Body and Blood to the priests of the Church. Help me see you in them and bless you for them. Give me the spirit and virtues I need to venerate them and offer them my honor, understanding, and support.

ADVENT ACTION

Write down the names of priests you know, particularly those in need of help and encouragement in their pastoral ministry. Look at the list regularly and remember them in prayer. Try to see the Lord working in and through them.

Creation and Sacraments

*H*ow is it that God has chosen us for something so great?
It's because He ordinarily uses the most inferior materials
for the extraordinary workings of His grace, as in the sacraments,
where He makes use of water and words to confer His greatest graces.

CONFERENCE 7

SCRIPTURE

For as often as you eat this bread and drink the cup, you proclaim the death of the Lord until he comes. Therefore whoever eats the bread or drinks the cup of the Lord unworthily will have to answer for the body and blood of the Lord. A person should examine himself, and so eat the bread and drink the cup.

1 CORINTHIANS 11:26–28

PRAYER

Father, how great is the ministry you have confided to your Church, and how simple the means! Help me pierce the sacramental mysteries we celebrate so I can see both the human and the divine, particularly in the holy Eucharist. Fill me with wonder for your love.

ADVENT ACTION

Before Mass, get into the habit of asking yourself: What specific intention am I going to pray for at today's Mass? Afterward, ask yourself regularly, Did I *really* pray at this Mass, or did I mainly attend out of duty or precept, even perhaps without a sense of the Lord's presence?

DAY 18

Enlightenment

*T*he lights of grace, which the Sun of Justice spreads in our souls, reveal and penetrate to the very depths and most intimate part of our heart, which they stir up and prompt to produce marvelous things. So then, we have to ask God to be himself the one to enlighten and inspire us with what is pleasing to Him.

CONFERENCE 69

SCRIPTURE

He explores the wisdom of all the ancients
and is occupied with the prophecies;
If it pleases the Lord Almighty,
he will be filled with the spirit of understanding;
He will pour forth his words of wisdom
and in prayer give praise to the Lord.

SIRACH 39:1, 6

PRAYER

God, creator of light, send that same light into my heart. Reveal my heart's hidden depths, and give me the energy to respond completely to your invitations to greater love. Cleanse all that is dark and unworthy of you, that I may more and more strive to do only what is pleasing to you.

ADVENT ACTION

The human heart is always a mixture of light and darkness. Today, pray for enlightenment while concentrating on the light the Sun of Justice has shown in your heart recently. Thank him for that brilliance, ask him for strength to continue, and ask his forgiveness for responding incompletely to his enlightenment. Plan to celebrate the enlightenment you've received by witnessing to it with word and action.

DAY 19

The Presence of God

*G*od is an abyss of perfections, an eternal, very holy, very pure, very perfect, and infinitely glorious Being, an infinite Good who encompasses all goods and is incomprehensible in himself.

CONFERENCE 30

SCRIPTURE

> *Blessed be the LORD, my rock,…*
> *My safeguard and my fortress,*
> *my stronghold, my deliverer,*
> *My shield, in whom I take refuge,*
> *who subdues peoples under me.*

LORD, what is man that you take notice of him;
the son of man, that you think of him?
Man is but a breath,
his days are like a passing shadow.

PSALM 144:1–4

PRAYER

God of all perfection, give me the light to see your hand in everything that I do. Send your Holy Spirit into my heart to fill me with love and gratitude for life and for your guiding hand. May my earthly life grow in imitation of your perfection so that I may one day share heavenly life with you.

ADVENT ACTION

Saint Vincent de Paul was given to action for the poor and marginalized, and he spent untold hours attending meetings and writing letters. Yet he was grounded in contemplation, as today's passage relates. Today as you begin a new task, ask, *Where is my center? What gives me life?* Find a few moments—even in the most ordinary work—to ask the same questions. Hold on to the answers so you can record them in your journal later.

DAY 20

Reliance on God

*W*hat do you think is most often the cause of our failing in our resolutions? It's that we depend too much on ourselves, we put our trust in our good desires, we rely on our own strength, and that's the reason we don't get any good results from them.

CONFERENCE 70

SCRIPTURE

More tortuous than all else is the human heart,
beyond remedy; who can understand it?
I, the Lord, alone probe the mind
and test the heart,

To reward everyone according to his ways,
according to the merit of his deeds.
A partridge that mothers a brood not her own
is the man who acquires wealth unjustly:
In midlife it will desert him;
in the end he is only a fool.

JEREMIAH 17:9–11

PRAYER

Father, I come to you today aware of my failings. I often resolve to improve, to root out the deadly tendencies I see in myself, but I know I've failed. I bring you myself today in sacrifice and pray that henceforth I may rely on you alone, allowing you to cradle me in your loving embrace.

ADVENT ACTION

Saint Vincent was an acute observer of the human condition. He could see in himself and others the "dark side" of the human reality, yet he always returned to the Lord. Today, as you meditate in the quiet of the Advent season, focus on the realities of your heart, both light and dark. Offer yourself to God as you are, not as some ideal version of yourself. He made you, he understands you, and he alone probes the human heart to its depths. Celebrate the sacrament of reconciliation, and speak the truth you see in your actions.

DAY 21

On Valuing Learning

*O*Messieurs," he said, "who will give us this humility, which will sustain us! How hard it is to find a man who is really knowledgeable and truly humble! Nevertheless, they're not incompatible."

CONFERENCE 98

SCRIPTURE

> *The law of the LORD is perfect,*
> *refreshing the soul.*
> *The decree of the LORD is trustworthy,*
> *giving wisdom to the simple.*

The precepts of the LORD are right,
rejoicing the heart.
The command of the LORD is clear,
enlightening the eye.
The fear of the LORD is pure,
enduring forever.
The statutes of the LORD are true,
all of them just.

PSALM 19:8–10

PRAYER

I praise and thank you, Holy Spirit of God, for the experience and insights you've granted through my life. Help me use this knowledge for the good of your people, to help those who look to me for guidance and for an example of a truly Christ-centered life.

ADVENT ACTION

Saint Vincent's followers sometimes criticized him for underestimating learning. In fact, he encouraged it, but always within the framework of knowledge useful for salvation. Ask yourself during this meditative time of Advent how you're using your knowledge and experience. Are you merely showing it off? Can others deepen their faith because of your wisdom?

DAY 22

Waiting for Healing

*I*t must be admitted that the state of sickness is an unfortunate state and is almost unbearable to nature; nevertheless,
it's one of the most powerful means God uses to remind us of our
duty, to detach us from attraction to sin, and to fill us with His
gifts and graces.

CONFERENCE 55

SCRIPTURE

I was at the point of death,
my life was nearing the depths of Sheol;
I turned every way, but there was no one to help;
I looked for support but there was none.
Then I remembered the mercies of the LORD,
his acts of kindness through ages past;
For he saves those who take refuge in him,
and rescues them from every evil.

SIRACH 51:6–8

PRAYER

Lord Jesus, many people flocked to you for healing, but many others continued to be affected by illness of every sort. When illness strikes me, help me see your presence even there. May I come to appreciate my own mortality and weakness and take steps to grow in reliance on you.

ADVENT ACTION

If you have an illness, do you lash out at God for your sufferings? Try, instead, to accept whatever comes from the mighty and provident hand of God. Choose a family member or acquaintance who is ill and reach out to that person in prayer, but especially in human contact. Phone calls and texts work, but being there in person is infinitely more healing.

DAY 23

Prayer and Activity

*T*o recognize and discern [spiritual impulses], he noted that, with regard to impulses we feel for extraordinary things, we must always have recourse to spiritual directors; and for ordinary impulses, we should examine whether or not the inspiration was accompanied by haste because *non in commotione Dominus* ["the Lord is not in the earthquake"].

CONFERENCE 82A

SCRIPTURE

Then the LORD said [to Elijah]: Go out and stand on the mountain before the LORD; the LORD will pass by. There was a strong and violent wind rending the mountains and crushing rocks before the LORD—but the LORD was not in the wind; after the wind, an earthquake—but the LORD was not in the earthquake; after the earthquake, fire—but the LORD was not in the fire; after the fire, a light silent sound.

1 KINGS 19:11–12

PRAYER

Lord, grant me balance. I praise you for the lights you give me, and I repent for the times I haven't followed your call. Help me to listen more attentively and to follow you in the quiet and tranquility that are the hallmarks of the spiritual life.

ADVENT ACTION

Elijah the prophet experienced the Lord, but in a way he never expected. He thought rushing winds and the flash of lightning and thunder accompanied the Lord's coming. Instead, he found the Lord in the "light silent sound." Advent should be a time of listening and waiting. Pick a comfortable chair, light a candle, and spend a few minutes clearing your brain to wait for the Lord's voice. This is not automatic and may demand a consistent devotional practice to attain this awareness. Keep a log of what happens, and thank the Lord for everything.

DAY 24

Prayer and Graces

*G*od gives us His graces according to our needs. God is a fountain from which each of us draws water according to the need we have of it. Just as a person who needs six buckets of water draws six, and someone who needs three draws three, a bird, who needs only a billful, just dips in his beak, and a pilgrim scoops up a handful to slake his thirst. That's how God acts with us.

CONFERENCE 88

SCRIPTURE

Jesus answered [the Samaritan woman], "Everyone who drinks this water will be thirsty again; but whoever drinks the water I shall give will never thirst; the water I shall give will become in him a spring of water welling up to eternal life." The woman said to him, "Sir, give me this water, so that I may not be thirsty or have to keep coming here to draw water."

JOHN 4:13–15

PRAYER

God, almighty Father, you are the source of all blessings and graces. Others lead beautiful Christian lives, while my life is lacking in so many areas. Still, I put faith in you to grant me what I need according to your will for me. Ready me to receive your gifts.

ADVENT ACTION

God offers us the saints both for our imitation and comfort. We can imitate their spiritual strengths and take comfort in their difficulties. Sometimes these stemmed from their own characters. Saint Vincent de Paul began as a harsh and demanding person, but by the practice of virtue he became "the meekest man of his time." Reread the life of a favorite saint to see how the Lord granted his graces in his or her life. At a time of gift-giving, these are the great gifts you receive.

DAY 25

Eternal Truths

*O*nly eternal truths are capable of filling our hearts and of guiding us with assurance. Take my word for it, all we have to do is to rely strongly and solidly on one of the perfections of God, e.g., His goodness, His Providence, His truth, His immensity, etc.

CONFERENCE 18

SCRIPTURE

God also said: See, I give you every seed-bearing plant on all the earth and every tree that has seed-bearing fruit on it to be your food; and to all the wild animals, all the birds of the air, and all the living creatures that crawl on the earth, I give all the green plants for food. And so it happened. God looked at everything he had made, and found it very good. Evening came, and morning followed—the sixth day.

GENESIS 1:29–31

PRAYER

Help me, God, to place all my confidence in you. You've shown me in the holy Scriptures many examples of your goodness, your guiding hand, and your marvelous creativity. As I consider all of these, strengthen my faith and let me commit myself even more deeply to you.

ADVENT ACTION

On a clear winter's night, look up at the moon, the stars, and the planets. Our ancestors have done this for millennia before us, and all have been struck by their mysterious beauty. Look at them with the eyes of faith to see the God of all creation who set them in motion and keeps them in existence. Try to draw out from these considerations a more profound sense of the Lord's care for us.

DAY 26

God's Majesty

*L*et's strive to conceive a great—a very great—esteem for the majesty and holiness of God. If our mind's eye were powerful enough to penetrate ever so little into the immensity of His sovereign excellence, *Jésus!*, with what lofty sentiments we'd be filled!

CONFERENCE 30

SCRIPTURE

Not to us, LORD, not to us
but to your name give glory
because of your mercy and faithfulness.
Why should the nations say,
"Where is their God?"
Our God is in heaven
and does whatever he wills.

PSALM 115:1–3

PRAYER

Heavenly Father, lord of all creation, fill me with a deep sense of your majesty as I contemplate the mysteries of the universe and the inner harmony of the tiniest and most secret workings of life revealed through human science. As I look forward to the celebration of Jesus' birth, may I also see your love for me in the human life we share.

ADVENT ACTION

Take time out to look at something small and beautiful, and reflect on the majesty of the Creator who brought it all into being. Then concentrate on thanking the same Lord who gives life and sustains it in so many marvelous ways.

DAY 27

The Morning Offering

*L*et's take great care to offer our actions to God, especially the principal ones; and, even if, in our morning offering, we offer all the actions of the day to God, it's still good to offer each one in particular during the day.

CONFERENCE 117

SCRIPTURE

> *My heart is steadfast.*
> *I will sing and chant praise.*
> *Awake, my soul;*
> *awake, lyre and harp!*

I will wake the dawn.
I will praise you among the peoples, Lord;
I will chant your praise among the nations.
For your mercy towers to the heavens;
your faithfulness reaches to the skies.

PSALM 57:8–11

PRAYER

Heavenly Father, each day I want to offer to you all my actions. May I do them out of love for you and my brothers and sisters. Help me see that you're always present to me, offering me graces and blessings. May I in turn consecrate my life to you.

ADVENT ACTION

Our saint made it his practice to be always alert to the presence of God in daily life. At the beginning of each day, he turned his thoughts to God and offered the day to the glory of God. He often returned to this practice throughout the day. Make it your devotional practice to turn to the Lord often during the day, acknowledging his presence in your life, and begging him for the strength to accomplish the tasks at hand in his Spirit. At the end of the day, ask yourself how you did. Learn from your mistakes, and thank God for your successes. The approach of Christmas is especially timely as you reflect on God in your life.

Union Through Charity

ℬe united among yourselves and God will bless you; but let it be through the charity of Jesus Christ, for any other union that's not cemented by the Blood of this Divine Savior can't subsist. So, it's in Jesus Christ, through Jesus Christ, and for Jesus Christ that you must be united with one another.

CONFERENCE 104A

SCRIPTURE

At present we see indistinctly, as in a mirror, but then face to face. At present I know partially; then I shall know fully, as I am fully known. So faith, hope, love remain, these three; but the greatest of these is love.

1 CORINTHIANS 13:12–13

PRAYER

Lord Jesus Christ, through my baptism I have been joined to you in a profound spiritual union. Your death and rising to new life are *my* death and rising. May I never break those bonds through choosing myself over you, and thus may I live in you, through you, and for you. With this strength, help me to be united with my sisters and brothers, especially those in the greatest need. As Christmas approaches, purify me of all that would lessen this union with those closest to me.

ADVENT ACTION

Do you know the date of your baptism? Does it mean anything to you as an anniversary? If you were baptized as an adult, it should still have a profound presence. If you were baptized as an infant, check your baptismal certificate to find the date of your rebirth to new life in Christ and resolve to remember and celebrate it. It's another way to celebrate the birth of Jesus.

PART II

~~~

READINGS
for the
CHRISTMAS
SEASON

DAY 1

Animals Around the Crib

*T*hink about mules; are they proud because they're well har-nessed, laden with gold and silver, and adorned with beauti-ful plumes? In the same way, Messieurs, if we're praised or held in esteem—perhaps because we've performed some action that dazzled people—let's pay no attention to that, let's make no account of it.

CONFERENCE 120

SCRIPTURE

LORD, my heart is not proud;
nor are my eyes haughty.
I do not busy myself with great matters,
with things too sublime for me.
Rather, I have stilled my soul,
Like a weaned child to its mother,
weaned is my soul.

PSALM 131:1–2

PRAYER

All praise to you alone, O Lord. You are the source of all good and blessings. If I've accomplished anything in the years allotted to me, I give you thanks. Left to myself, I would have failed.

CHRISTMAS ACTION

As you pray before the crib in this Christmas season, take a look at the animals that traditionally surround the Holy Family. Saint Vincent was much more aware of mules than we are, because in his day they were often the beasts of burden for the wealthy and the nobles. The mules didn't care what they carried. Put yourself in the place of the mules around the crib, privileged to see the events there, but destined for something they couldn't plan for. Bless the Lord for whatever burden he asks you to carry.

Jesus Our Model

*O*ur Lord Jesus Christ is the true model and that great invisible portrait on whom we must fashion all our actions. The most perfect men living here below on earth are the visible, tangible pictures who serve as models for us to regulate all our actions well and make them pleasing to God.

CONFERENCE 128

SCRIPTURE

So whether you eat or drink, or whatever you do, do everything for the glory of God. Avoid giving offense, whether to Jews or Greeks or the church of God, just as I try to please everyone in every way, not seeking my own benefit but that of the many, that they may be saved. Be imitators of me, as I am of Christ.

1 CORINTHIANS 10:31—11:1

PRAYER

God our Father, I praise you for the gift of your Son, Jesus, whom the Church celebrates in this season. As I contemplate his life, from a simple stable birth to his death and resurrection, may I be filled with the desire to imitate him in my daily life.

CHRISTMAS ACTION

The Christmas season can offer you moments to think about the birth of Jesus as well as the good, generous, self-giving people in your life. Reflect on one aspect of Jesus' birth—his confidence in Mary, his gentleness, his readiness to give himself for others—and draw out a lesson for yourself. Think too about another person you esteem. Make a mental or written note about the quality you'd most like to imitate in the year ahead.

DAY 3

Pure Love of God

*I*s there any risk in loving God? Can we love Him too much? Can there be any excess in something so holy and divine? Can we ever have sufficient love for God, who is infinitely loveable? It's true that we can never love God enough and can never go to excess in this love if we consider what God deserves from us.

CONFERENCE 129

SCRIPTURE

I urge you therefore, brothers, by the mercies of God, to offer your bodies as a living sacrifice, holy and pleasing to God, your spiritual worship. Do not conform yourselves to this age but be transformed by the renewal of your mind, that you may discern what is the will of God, what is good and pleasing and perfect.

ROMANS 12:1–2

PRAYER

Heavenly Father, Creator God, help me grow in my love of you. Transform me in this way. May my life, lived in accord with your will, be my loving sacrifice to you in thanksgiving for the love you show me.

CHRISTMAS ACTION

The great gift of Christmas—the gift symbolized by all the other gifts given in this season—is the person of Jesus, offered in love. For your daily devotion today, offer God your thanks for this gift of his love, and then reflect on what you can do to make your loving response more real and heartfelt during this season.

DAY 4

Balanced Virtues

*V*irtue always lies in the middle, my dear confreres; each virtue has two vicious extremes; no matter from which side we happen to move away, we fall into one of these faults; for our actions to be praiseworthy, we have to walk a straight line between those two extremes.

CONFERENCE 129

SCRIPTURE

On the way of wisdom I direct you,
I lead you on straight paths.
Hold fast to instruction, never let it go;
keep it, for it is your life.
The path of the wicked do not enter,
nor walk in the way of the evil;
But the path of the just is like shining light,
that grows in brilliance till perfect day.

PROVERBS 4:11, 13–14, 18

PRAYER

Father of Our Lord Jesus Christ, in these days after the celebration of his birth, your Church begins to present our Savior growing in virtue. As I am born anew into his body, the Church, help me also to grow in virtue. Through the light of your Holy Spirit, may I always find the right path and follow it wholeheartedly.

CHRISTMAS ACTION

Saint Vincent calls his followers to walk with prudence and forethought. You may have time during the hectic days after Christmas to look to your own growth into deeper Christian life. Try to imitate and thereby honor the virtues practiced by the Son of God that you need most in your own life. Pick one, look for it in Jesus' life, and resolve to follow him in this practice.

DAY 5

Communion With the Newborn Savior

When God wants to communicate himself, He does it effortlessly, in a perceptible, very pleasant, gentle, loving way; so, let's ask Him often and with great confidence for this gift of meditation. On His part, God asks for nothing better; let's pray to Him, but let's do it with great confidence.

CONFERENCE 129

SCRIPTURE

When the angels went away from them to heaven, the shepherds said to one another, "Let us go, then, to Bethlehem to see this thing that has taken place, which the Lord has made known to us." So they went in haste and found Mary and Joseph, and the infant lying in the manger. When they saw this, they made known the message that had been told them about this child. All who heard it were amazed by what had been told them by the shepherds. And Mary kept all these things, reflecting on them in her heart.

LUKE 2:15–19

PRAYER

God of majesty and power, you are the creator of all, including the far reaches of space and the innermost workings of atoms. Yet you communicate gently and sweetly with those you call. Grant me that gift of communication with you through quiet prayer, and surround me with your peace.

CHRISTMAS ACTION

Nothing is hurried or abrupt in the account of the birth of Jesus. Contemplate today the Blessed Virgin Mary, who is now a mother. After the visit of shepherds and wise men, she treasures all these events in her heart. Ask yourself what you treasure in *your* heart. Keep the good, and try to rid yourself of whatever can disrupt your peace of soul.

DAY 6

Freedom Amid Plenty

*O*h, if God were to grant us the grace of opening the curtain that prevents us from seeing such beauty [the virtue of poverty]; if only He were to lift, by His grace, all the veils that the world and our self-love cast before our eyes, Messieurs, we'd be immediately delighted with the charms of that virtue which delighted the heart and affections of the Son of God!

CONFERENCE 132

SCRIPTURE

Do not store up for yourselves treasures on earth, where moth and decay destroy, and thieves break in and steal. But store up treasures in heaven, where neither moth nor decay destroys, nor thieves break in and steal. For where your treasure is, there also will your heart be.

MATTHEW 6:19–21

PRAYER

Lord Jesus, you came down among us as a man. Your entire life, from your birth in Bethlehem to your death and rising, calls me to examine what is truly valuable in my life and what is only accessory. Give me the insight to value everything in the light of your truth.

CHRISTMAS ACTION

The Christmas season, more than any other, calls us to reflect on the value of things. Take a look around your house or living area today, and ask yourself what you could do without. What is superfluous? What would you do if you lost certain prized possessions through some accident? Keep a list of the answers. As you examine the life of Jesus, born in a stable, try to live more simply.

DAY 7

Detachment and Attachment

*A*long with our possessions, we must also give up the attachment and love of possessions, and have no love for the perishable goods of this world. It's doing nothing, it's making a mockery of an exterior renunciation of goods, if we hold on to the desire to have them. God asks primarily for our heart—our heart—and that's what counts.

CONFERENCE 132

SCRIPTURE

He said to [his] disciples, "Therefore I tell you, do not worry about your life and what you will eat, or about your body and what you will wear. For life is more than food and the body more than clothing. Notice the ravens: they do not sow or reap; they have neither storehouse nor barn, yet God feeds them. How much more important are you than birds! Can any of you by worrying add a moment to your lifespan?

LUKE 12:22–25

PRAYER

Almighty God, you are Lord of all things, of all times, and seasons. At the end of this year, with its mixture of good and evil, help me focus once again on you, the source of all blessings. May I be detached from the things of this Earth and always pine for you alone.

CHRISTMAS ACTION

The old year is closing. Saint Vincent wanted his followers to spend the day in a retreat to give thanksgiving for the past year, make reparation for sins and failings, and prepare for the new year. Take extra time today to be peaceful. Find a quiet space, a comfortable chair, and relax by breathing deeply. Slowly call to mind the major events of the year. Are you more attached to the Lord now than you were a year ago? Have you truly given your heart to the Lord?

DAY 8

God's Care for Us

*T*oday the subject of our meditation is the love of God and the reasons we have to love God. Alas, Brothers, we don't have to look for many reasons to excite us to this love! We don't have to go outside ourselves to find any; we have only to consider the good things He's done for us and continues to do for us daily. And to oblige us even further, He has commanded us to do it. You see that this subject of itself sets our will afire.

CONFERENCE 133

SCRIPTURE

My soul yearns and pines
for the courts of the LORD.
My heart and flesh cry out
for the living God.
As the sparrow finds a home
and the swallow a nest to settle her young,
My home is by your altars,
LORD of hosts, my king and my God!

PSALM 84:3–4

PRAYER

Father, on this New Year's Day, I make my own the prayer of the psalmist. I cry out for a deeper sense of your presence. In the year beginning today, grant me the grace to sense that my home, my life, my future is in you. Give me the joy and peace promised in this Christmas season.

CHRISTMAS ACTION

New Year's Day is traditionally a time for resolutions for the year that opens before us. This year, on the spiritual path, resolve to be ever more conscious of the loving presence of God. A traditional way to help people remember this was to rely on the bells that rang regularly throughout the day in towns and villages. Choose something that regularly occurs throughout your day, like mealtimes, to center your attention.

DAY 9

Following the Son of God

*I*t's a necessity for anyone who wants to follow the Son of God to become perfect; he must leave everything. *Vade, vende omnia quae habes et da pauperibus* ["Go, sell what you have and give to the poor"]. It's the first of the beatitudes; it's the legacy the Son of God left to His dear children in this world.

CONFERENCE 132

SCRIPTURE

When he saw the crowds, he went up the mountain, and after he had sat down, his disciples came to him. He began to teach them, saying: "Blessed are the poor in spirit, for theirs is the kingdom of heaven."

MATTHEW 5:1–3

PRAYER

Lord Jesus, your public ministry began with words proclaiming that the poor in spirit are blessed. To follow you in this new year, I must put aside any selfish care of myself, emptying myself to be filled with you. Give me strength and nourish me by the food of the holy Eucharist so that, with eyes and heart fixed on you, I may become your true disciple.

CHRISTMAS ACTION

Being poor in spirit is more profound than being poor in goods or intellectual or social resources. It means emptying yourself of whatever hinders you from being filled with God. Take some time today to look into the hidden corners God doesn't enter. Offer this to the Lord as your gift, and beg him to fill you with himself.

DAY 10

God's Eternal Purposes

*W*hen the Divine Majesty grants us the grace of getting to heaven above, one of the first things God will show us will be the reasons why He acted the way He did on earth; for you see, God does nothing without some good purpose and only very justly; that's why we must be conformed to His Will in everything and adore His ever-admirable guidance, although these are often unknown to us and we'll never know them until we get to heaven.

CONFERENCE 140

SCRIPTURE

Who has directed the spirit of the LORD,
or instructed him as his counselor?
Whom did he consult to gain knowledge?
Who taught him the path of judgment,
or showed him the way of understanding?
See, the nations count as a drop in the bucket,
as a wisp of cloud on the scales;
the coastlands weigh no more than a speck.

ISAIAH 40:13–15

PRAYER

Almighty Father, you are Lord of all things, and your thoughts are beyond all human understanding. When the world fills me with doubt or disillusion, grant me the peace and contentment the infant Jesus felt in his mother's arms. Help me put myself in your hands with all confidence.

CHRISTMAS ACTION

One of Saint Vincent's most common expressions was "give yourself to God." As you think about the meaning of Christmas and ponder the life that Jesus would live on Earth, pray as well about your own life's twists and turns. Can you see the hand of God? It's helpful to list events you didn't foresee but in which you can now see God's loving guidance. Praise the Creator for this care for you.

DAY 11

The Humility of the Child Jesus

What convinces us more strongly of this truth [humility] is our natural, constant inclination to evil, our powerlessness to do good, and the experience all of us have that, even when we think we've succeeded well in some action or that our advice has been well received, just the opposite happens, and God often allows us to be held in contempt.

CONFERENCE 38

SCRIPTURE

In the beginning was the Word, and the Word was with God,
and the Word was God. He was in the beginning with God.
And the Word became flesh and made his dwelling among us,
and we saw his glory, the glory as of the Father's only Son, full
of grace and truth.

JOHN 1:1–2, 14

PRAYER

God our Father, I praise and thank you in this Christmas
season for the birth among us of Jesus, your Son. Although
I'm tempted to think of this little child as merely human or
only a symbol of your presence, I can peer more deeply with
the light of your Holy Spirit. Help me to grasp what I celebrate
in these days: the Word made flesh, living among us.

CHRISTMAS ACTION

Saint Vincent was an acute observer of the human condition.
Through his own meditation, he perceived his own weak-
nesses. As you look forward, consider the challenges facing
you in this new year. Ponder your own history, and name
those times when you failed to live up to your highest hopes.
Give yourself to God humbly, admitting your imperfections,
and beg for healing.

DAY 12

Reverence for Christ

Oh bien, my dear confreres! Let's strive then to perform this action properly, to make inclinations and genuflections well; for example, to genuflect properly, then to bow, when we walk in a procession.

CONFERENCE 119

SCRIPTURE

I saw the Lord seated on a high and lofty throne, with the train of his garment filling the temple. Seraphim were stationed above...."Holy, holy, holy is the Lord of hosts! All the earth is filled with his glory!" At the sound of that cry, the frame of the door shook and the house was filled with smoke.

ISAIAH 6:1–4

PRAYER

Lord Jesus Christ, remove from me the temptation to take the faith, the Church, and its sacraments for granted. Give me instead a deep reverence for holy things. May this sense of your presence in Word and Eucharist transform my behavior into that which proclaims my faith in you.

CHRISTMAS ACTION

Familiarity, even with matters of religion, can breed contempt in the sense of valuing the holiest of things lightly. The next time you enter a church, try to focus on the Lord who is present there and on the life-giving sacraments celebrated there. Great moments of life and death can move us deeply, but daily or weekly Mass attendance can leave us uninvolved. Try instead to move to a deeper level of consciousness of God's presence in the celebration of the holy liturgy.

PART III

~~~~~

FORMATS

for

NIGHTLY
PRAYER

and

READING

Formats for Nightly Prayer and Reading

THE PURPOSE OF PRESENTING two optional formats for nightly reading and prayer is to offer ways to use the material in this book for group or individual prayer. Of course, there are other ways in which to use this book—for example, as a meditative daily reader or as a guide for a prayer journal—but the following familiar liturgical formats provide a structure that can be used in a variety of contexts.

FORMAT 1

OPENING PRAYER

The observance begins with these words:

> God, come to my assistance.
> Lord, make haste to help me.

followed by:

> Glory to the Father, and to the Son,
> and to the Holy Spirit, as it was in the beginning,
> is now, and will be for ever. Amen. Alleluia.

EXAMINATION OF CONSCIENCE

If this observance is being prayed individually, an examination of conscience may be included. Here is a short examination of conscience; you may, of course, use your own method.

1. Place yourself in a quiet frame of mind.

2. Review your life since your last confession.

3. Reflect on the Ten Commandments and any sins against these commandments.

4. Reflect on the words of the gospel, especially Jesus' commandment to love your neighbor as yourself.

5. Ask yourself these questions: Have I been unkind in thoughts, words, and actions? Am I refusing to forgive anyone? Do I despise any group or person? Am I a prisoner of fear, anxiety, worry, guilt, inferiority, or hatred of myself?

PENITENTIAL RITE (OPTIONAL)

If a group of people are praying in unison, a penitential rite from *The Roman Missal* may be used:

Presider: You were sent to heal the contrite of heart:
Lord, have mercy.
All: Lord, have mercy.
Presider: You came to call sinners:
Christ, have mercy.
All: Christ, have mercy.
Presider: You are seated at the right hand of the Father to intercede for us:
Lord, have mercy.
All: Lord, have mercy.
Presider: May almighty God have mercy on us,
forgive us our sins,
and bring us to everlasting life.
All: Amen.

HYMN: "O COME, O COME, EMMANUEL"

A hymn is now sung or recited. This Advent hymn is a paraphrase of the great "O" Antiphons, written in the twelfth century and translated by John Mason Neale in 1852.

O come, O come, Emmanuel,
And ransom captive Israel;
That mourns in lonely exile here,
Until the Son of God appear.

Refrain: Rejoice! Rejoice! O Israel,
        To thee shall come Emmanuel!

O come, thou wisdom, from on high,
And order all things far and nigh;
To us the path of knowledge show,
And teach us in her ways to go. *(Refrain)*

O come, O come, thou Lord of might,
Who to thy tribes on Sinai's height
In ancient times did give the law,
In cloud, and majesty, and awe. *(Refrain)*

O come, thou rod of Jesse's stem,
From ev'ry foe deliver them
That trust thy mighty power to save,
And give them vict'ry o'er the grave. *(Refrain)*

O come, thou key of David, come,
And open wide our heav'nly home,
Make safe the way that leads on high,
That we no more have cause to sigh. *(Refrain)*

O come, thou Dayspring from on high,
And cheer us by thy drawing nigh;
Disperse the gloomy clouds of night
And death's dark shadow put to flight. *(Refrain)*

O come, Desire of nations, bind
In one the hearts of all mankind;
Bid every strife and quarrel cease
And fill the world with heaven's peace. *(Refrain)*

PSALM 27:7–14 GOD STANDS BY US IN DANGERS

Hear my voice, LORD, when I call;
have mercy on me and answer me.
"Come," says my heart, "seek his face";
your face, LORD, do I seek!
Do not hide your face from me;
do not repel your servant in anger.
You are my salvation; do not cast me off;
do not forsake me, God my savior!
Even if my father and mother forsake me,
the LORD will take me in.
LORD, show me your way;
lead me on a level path
because of my enemies.
Do not abandon me to the desire of my foes;
malicious and lying witnesses have risen against me.
I believe I shall see the LORD's goodness
in the land of the living.
Wait for the LORD, take courage;
be stouthearted, wait for the LORD!

RESPONSE

I long to see your face, O Lord. You are my light and my help.
Do not turn away from me.

SCRIPTURE READING

Read silently or have a presider proclaim the Scripture of the day that is selected.

RESPONSE

Come and set us free, Lord God of power and might. Let your face shine on us and we will be saved.

Glory to the Father, and to the Son,
and to the Holy Spirit:
as it was in the beginning, is now,
and will be for ever. Amen.

SECOND READING

Read silently or have a presider read the words of Saint Vincent de Paul for the day selected.

CANTICLE OF SIMEON

Lord, now you let your servant go in peace;
    your word has been fulfilled:
my own eyes have seen the salvation
    which you have prepared in the sight of every people:
a light to reveal you to the nations
    and the glory of your people Israel.
Glory to the Father, and to the Son, and to the Holy Spirit:
as it was in the beginning, is now,
and will be for ever. Amen.

PRAYER

Recite the prayer that follows the excerpt from Saint Vincent de Paul for the day selected.

BLESSING

May the all-powerful Lord grant us a restful night and a peaceful death. Amen.

MARIAN ANTIPHON

Loving mother of the Redeemer,
gate of heaven, star of the sea,
assist your people who have fallen yet strive to rise again.
To the wonderment of nature you bore your Creator,
yet remained a virgin after as before.
You who received Gabriel's joyful greeting,
have pity on us poor sinners.

FORMAT 2

OPENING PRAYER

The observance begins with these words:

God, come to my assistance.
Lord, make haste to help me.

followed by

Glory to the Father, and to the Son,
and to the Holy Spirit, as it was in the beginning,
is now, and will be for ever. Amen. Alleluia.

EXAMINATION OF CONSCIENCE

If this observance is being prayed individually, an examination of conscience may be included. Here is a short examination of conscience; you may, of course, use your own method.

1. Place yourself in a quiet frame of mind.

2. Review your life since your last confession.

3. Reflect on the Ten Commandments and any sins against these commandments.

4. Reflect on the words of the gospel, especially Jesus' commandment to love your neighbor as yourself.

5. Ask yourself these questions: Have I been unkind in thoughts, words, and actions? Am I refusing to forgive anyone? Do I despise any group or person? Am I a prisoner of fear, anxiety, worry, guilt, inferiority, or hatred of myself?

PENITENTIAL RITE (OPTIONAL)

If a group of people are praying in unison, a penitential rite from the *Roman Missal* may be used:

All: I confess to almighty God
           and to you, my brothers and sisters,
           that I have greatly sinned,
           in my thoughts and in my words,
           in what I have done and in what I have failed to do,

And, striking their breast, they say:
           through my fault, through my fault,
           through my most grievous fault;

Then they continue:
           therefore I ask blessed Mary ever-Virgin,
           all the Angels and Saints,
           and you, my brothers and sisters,
           to pray for me to the Lord our God.

Presider: May almighty God have mercy on us,
             forgive us our sins,
             and bring us to everlasting life.

All: Amen.

HYMN: "BEHOLD, A ROSE"

A hymn is now sung or recited. This traditional hymn was composed in German in the fifteenth century. It is sung to the melody of the familiar "Lo, How a Rose E're Blooming."

> Behold, a rose of Judah
> From tender branch has sprung,
> From Jesse's lineage coming,
> As men of old have sung.
> It came a flower bright
> Amid the cold of winter
> When half spent was the night.
> Isaiah has foretold it
> In words of promise sure,
> And Mary's arms enfold it,
> A virgin meek and pure.
> Through God's eternal will
> She bore for men a savior
> At midnight calm and still.

PSALM 40:2–8 THANKSGIVING FOR DELIVERANCE

> Surely, I wait for the LORD;
> who bends down to me and hears my cry,
> Draws me up from the pit of destruction,
> out of the muddy clay,
> Sets my feet upon rock,
> steadies my steps,
> And puts a new song in my mouth,
> a hymn to our God.

Many shall look on in fear
and they shall trust in the LORD.
Blessed the man who sets
his security in the LORD,
who turns not to the arrogant
or to those who stray after falsehood.
You, yes you, O LORD, my God,
have done many wondrous deeds!
And in your plans for us
there is none to equal you.
Should I wish to declare or tell them,
too many are they to recount.
Sacrifice and offering you do not want;
you opened my ears.
Holocaust and sin-offering you do not request;
so I said, "See; I come
with an inscribed scroll written upon me.

RESPONSE

May all who seek after you be glad in the Lord, may those
who find your salvation say with continuous praise, "Great
is the Lord!"

SCRIPTURE READING

Read silently or have a presider proclaim the Scripture of the day that is selected.

RESPONSE

Lord, you who were made obedient unto death, teach us to always do the Father's will so that, sanctified by the holy obedience that joins us to your sacrifice, we can count on your immense love in times of sorrow.

Glory to the Father, and to the Son,
and to the Holy Spirit:
as it was in the beginning, is now,
and will be for ever. Amen.

SECOND READING

Read silently or have a presider read the words of Saint Vincent de Paul for the day selected.

CANTICLE OF SIMEON

Lord, now you let your servant go in peace;
> your word has been fulfilled:
my own eyes have seen the salvation
> which you have prepared in the sight of every people:
a light to reveal you to the nations
> and the glory of your people Israel.

Glory to the Father, and to the Son,
and to the Holy Spirit:
as it was in the beginning, is now,
and will be for ever. Amen.

PRAYER

Recite the prayer that follows the excerpt from Saint Vincent de Paul for the day selected.

BLESSING

Lord, give our bodies restful sleep and let the work we have done today bear fruit in eternal life. Watch over us as we rest in your peace. Amen.

MARIAN ANTIPHON

Hail, holy Queen, mother of mercy,
>   our life, our sweetness, and our hope.
To you do we cry,
>   poor banished children of Eve.
To you do we send up our sighs,
>   mourning and weeping in this vale of tears.
Turn then, most gracious advocate,
>   your eyes of mercy toward us,
>   and after this exile
>   show to us the blessed fruit of your womb, Jesus.
O clement, O loving,
O sweet Virgin Mary. Amen.

CPSIA information can be obtained
at www.ICGtesting.com
Printed in the USA
LVHW01s1205211018
594309LV00022B/1543/P